This is a Carlton Book

Text, design and illustration copyright © Carlton Books Ltd 2016

Published in 2016 by Carlton Books Limited. An imprint of the Carlton Publishing Group, 20 Mortimer Street, London, W1T 3JW.

A catalog record for this book is available from the British Library.

ISBN: 978 1 78312 247 9

Printed in Dongguan, China

Author: Anna Brett
Editor: Tasha Percy
Design Director: Russell Porter
Design: WildPixel Ltd.
Production: Charlotte Larcombe

Picture Credits
All illustrations kindly supplied by Istockphoto.com and Shutterstock.com with the exception of the following:
26-27. John Hughes/Getty Images & 28-29. Dorling Kindersley/Getty Images.

Carlton Books Limited apologizes for any unintentional errors or omissions which will be corrected in future editions of this book.

NOTE TO PARENTS:
Need some help? Check out the instructions on the next page and our useful website: www.icarlton.co.uk/help

DINOSAUR BATTLE!

© Disney

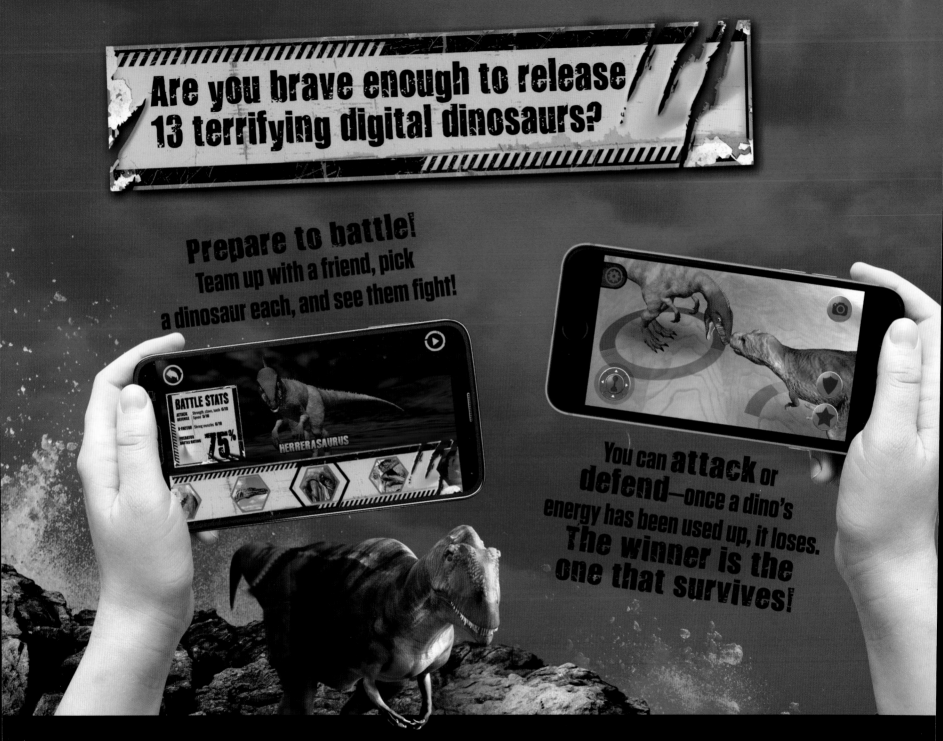

Are you brave enough to release 13 terrifying digital dinosaurs?

Prepare to battle!
Team up with a friend, pick a dinosaur each, and see them fight!

BATTLE STATS
ATTACK: Strength, claws, teeth 6/10
DEFENCE: Speed 5/10
X-FACTOR: Strong muscles 6/10
PREDATOR BATTLE RATING **75%**
HERRERASAURUS

You can **attack** or **defend**—once a dino's energy has been used up, it loses. **The winner is the one that survives!**

HOW IT WORKS

1. Download the FREE APP Dinosaur Battle from www.apple.com/itunes or www.android.com/apps and open it on your mobile device.

2. Each dino has its own activation page. Hold your device over one of the pages to release each fearsome beast in SINGLE USER mode.

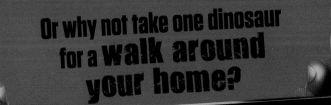

Or why not take one dinosaur for a **walk around** your home?

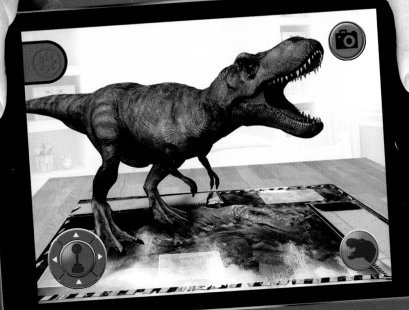

Take a picture, or make it **ROAR!**

Powered by **Digital Magic®**
This product will work with the following devices:
- The following Apple devices running iOS 7.0 or above: iPhone 5 or above; iPad3 or above; iPod Touch 5th Gen. or above.
- Android devices with both forward- and backward-facing cameras using Android 4.0 and above, and ARM NEON processors—INTEL based devices are not supported.
- Battle mode will require an active wi-fi connection.

3. In BATTLE MODE, grab a friend with a device. Open the app on both devices and select Battle Mode. User 1 taps the START button, selects their dino, then taps the PLAY button twice. Then they view THESE pages to activate their dino in the battle arena.

4. User 2 taps the START button, selects their dinosaur and taps the PLAY button. They then select the first user's device from the list of friends shown and views THESE pages to start the battle.

UTAHRAPTOR

This carnivorous creature didn't have to rely on its jaws and teeth to attack—it had two huge dangerous hooked claws on its feet to slash at prey. Combined with a quick top speed, this dinosaur was a terrifying predator.

FEATHERS, NOT FUR

Being covered in feathers provided Utahraptor with camouflage in the woods where it hunted. It had a fan of feathers growing out of its bony tail to help it balance—very useful for when it was standing on one foot and using the other to kick or stab its prey.

STAB AND SLICE

Utahraptor's sickle-shaped claws on the second toe of each foot were up to 10 inches long. These deadly weapons were used like a knife to stab at prey, and the hooked shape meant they could slice flesh off a carcass with one swift move.

SPEED OVER SIZE

At only 23 feet long, this dinosaur wasn't going to beat the likes of T. rex or Giganotosaurus for sheer presence. But its short, muscular legs gave it power and speed—a deadly combo when pursuing prey.

DINO BATTLE
☆ CONTENDER No.1 ☆

NAME	UTAHRAPTOR
	(YOU-tah-RAP-ter)
LENGTH	23 feet
WEIGHT	1,543 pounds
SPEED	30 mph

KEY ATTACKING MOVES
- Speed • Claw stab

BATTLE STATS

ATTACK	Claws, jaws **7/10**
DEFENSE	Speed, camouflage **8/10**
X-FACTOR	Two huge claws on feet **8/10**

PREDATOR BATTLE RATING

88%

SERRATED TEETH

A powerful jaw filled with teeth is only good if you know how to use it! Utahraptor's teeth were serrated, meaning they could saw through thick chunks of meat it had sliced off prey with its claws.

TYRANNOSAURUS REX

Does the king of the dinosaurs deserve such a title? Huge jaws, pointed teeth, thick tail, powerful muscles, and sharp claws—lots of predators share these features. What makes T. rex the undisputed king was its ferocious killer attitude.

CLEVER CARNIVORE

T. rex was smart. It knew what it was doing, and its ruthless attitude was combined with acute hearing and excellent eyesight. No other dinosaur could outsmart T. rex, and this is why it remains one of the deadliest predators that ever lived.

SENSE OF SMELL

Scientists have recently discovered that T. rex had a superior sense of smell. This meant it was likely to hunt at night as well as during the day, and it could navigate through large areas by sniffing out its next victim. It seems that there really was nowhere to hide for the prey of this fearsome beast.

POWERFUL GRIP

Although its arms were short, size doesn't always matter. The powerful grip and sharp claws these arms supported meant that they were a secret weapon, used for holding down prey or slashing through skin.

HEADS UP

Tyrannosaurus rex's head was its most striking feature. It had huge shoulder muscles to support the weight of its heavy head. While its teeth were on show, the real power was hidden away—the roof of its mouth was made of thick, hard bone and helped to create that mega-bite.

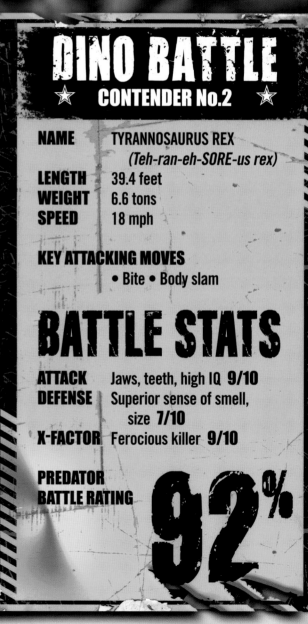

DINO BATTLE
★ CONTENDER No.2 ★

NAME	TYRANNOSAURUS REX
	(Teh-ran-eh-SORE-us rex)
LENGTH	39.4 feet
WEIGHT	6.6 tons
SPEED	18 mph

KEY ATTACKING MOVES
- Bite • Body slam

BATTLE STATS

ATTACK Jaws, teeth, high IQ **9/10**
DEFENSE Superior sense of smell, size **7/10**
X-FACTOR Ferocious killer **9/10**

PREDATOR BATTLE RATING **92%**

SPINOSAURUS

This huge predator is up for the award of biggest and best. With the speed of a T. rex, the jaws of a crocodile, and the body length of two buses, Spinosaurus had a killer combination of weapons.

SUPER SAIL

You wouldn't miss this dinosaur heading towards you with the supersized sail on its back. Scientists think the sail was used to help control body temperature, since blood could flow close to the surface of the skin here to warm up or cool down. It also made this dinosaur very intimidating!

LEGS AND CLAWS

Like other theropods, Spinosaurus walked on its two back legs. These powerful limbs meant that it could run at speeds of up to 20 mph. Its forearms were also long enough to enable it to walk on all fours, unlike T. rex. At the end of each limb were three sharp claws that were hooked so they could tear off chunks of meat.

TEETH AND JAWS

Spinosaurus's jaws were its primary weapon. Its head could grow up to 6 feet long, meaning it could easily grab prey with one bite. The jaw was lined with long, sharp teeth—perfect for holding on to slippery fish as it moved through the swamps.

LAND AND WATER

Spinosaurus lived in North Africa, on land that is now Egypt and Morocco. Its status as a top predator comes from the fact that it felt at home in the water as well as on land. It could often be found wading through swamps and lagoons, so there was no easy escape for prey.

DINO BATTLE
★ **CONTENDER No.3** ★

NAME	SPINOSAURUS *(Spine-oh-SORE-us)*
LENGTH	59.1 feet
WEIGHT	11 tons
SPEED	20 mph

KEY ATTACKING MOVES
• Bite • Claw swipe

BATTLE STATS

ATTACK	Claws, jaws	**9/10**
DEFENSE	Size, able to swim	**10/10**
X-FACTOR	Huge sail on back	**9/10**

PREDATOR BATTLE RATING  96%

VELOCIRAPTOR

Velociraptor was fearless—a good thing when you're a tiny predator playing with the big boys. Its speed, aggression, and sharp, hooked claws more than made up for its lack of size.

RAPID ATTACK

With a top speed of 25 mph, Velociraptor could approach prey swiftly and suddenly before its victim had even spotted any danger. Small and agile, this dinosaur was found darting around the open plains of eastern Asia.

DEADLY DAGGERS

The two sickle-shaped claws on the third toe of each foot were like daggers. Velociraptor could lift them off the ground when running, and then—in one quick movement—leap onto its prey and insert the daggers, creating a terrible wound.

NIGHT VISION

Velociraptor's eyes were adapted for hunting in low light. Fossils show that it had the same eye shape and size as modern animals that prowl at night. This meant it could hunt when it had the cover of darkness to protect it from larger beasts.

BIRD-LIKE LOOKS

Velociraptor had a long, low, flat skull and an upturned snout. Its 60 teeth were small and sharp—perfect for tearing flesh. Its body was covered in short feathers, with longer ones on the arms and tail. But you can be sure it was a dinosaur, not a bird!

DINO BATTLE
★ CONTENDER No.4 ★

NAME	VELOCIRAPTOR
	(Veh-LAHS-ee-rap-ter)
LENGTH	6.6 feet
WEIGHT	33 pounds
SPEED	25 mph

KEY ATTACKING MOVES

• Speed • Claw stab

BATTLE STATS

ATTACK	Claws, sharp teeth	6/10
DEFENSE	Speed, good eyesight	7/10
X-FACTOR	High IQ, group attack	8/10

PREDATOR BATTLE RATING 80%

MEGALOSAURUS

Its name means 'giant lizard' and it was the first dinosaur to be recognized by scientists. This predator is known for its powerful arms and strong grip, key features for a deadly killer.

BRITISH BEAST

Megalosaurus lived in the forests of what is now Great Britain during the Middle Jurassic Period. Trees and undergrowth meant that it could stalk its prey carefully before reaching out to grab, hold, and then deliver the bite.

BIG HEAD

A massive head and long jaws show that Megalosaurus was a classic carnivore. It had dagger-like teeth, ready to slice through flesh. A solid lower jaw suggests it had a bite to rival that of T. rex.

POWER GRIP

Megalosaurus would have been good at a tug of war—once it grabbed something, it didn't let go! Strong arms, longer than those of other dinosaurs, had three long claws at the end so that it could grab and pin down prey.

TWO OR FOUR?

When it was first discovered, scientists thought this dinosaur walked on four legs, like modern lizards. But like other predatory theropods ("beast-footed" dinosaurs), Megalosaurus actually walked on two legs, had a horizontal torso, and used its tail for balance.

DINO BATTLE
★ CONTENDER No.5 ★

NAME	MEGALOSAURUS
	(MEG-ah-lo-SORE-us)
LENGTH	19.7 feet
WEIGHT	1,543 pounds
SPEED	30 mph

KEY ATTACKING MOVES
• Bite • Strong grip

BATTLE STATS

ATTACK	Jaws, strength	6/10
DEFENSE	Speed	5/10
X-FACTOR	Powerful grip	7/10

PREDATOR BATTLE RATING 78%

HERRERASAURUS

Herrerasaurus was the number one dinosaur in South America during the Triassic Period. At 13 feet long it was the biggest beast in its class and it had the pick of the region's smaller dinosaurs.

MUSCLE WORKOUT

Big muscles don't come naturally, and early reptiles didn't all have strong, powerful bodies. Herrerasaurus marked the start of the rise of the mega-beasts—those with big muscles were better hunters and lived longer, so they were natural survivors.

DAYLIGHT SPRINTER

Scientists believe that Herrerasaurus was active during the day for short periods of time. With a top speed of 30 mph, this probably means it was a sprint champion.

RIVALS

Even the very top predators have rivals. Herrerasaurus's rival was Saurosuchus—a giant, crocodile-like reptile that was around 23 feet long and walked on all four legs.

CURVED TEETH

Herrerasaurus had 80 curved, serrated teeth. The serrations meant it could rip up flesh, and the curved teeth meant that if it grabbed prey whole, it wouldn't slide out of its mouth when running.

DINO BATTLE

☆ CONTENDER No.6 ☆

NAME	HERRERASAURUS
	(Her-AIR-uh-SORE-us)
LENGTH	13.1 feet
WEIGHT	441 pounds
SPEED	30 mph

KEY ATTACKING MOVES

• Claw swipe • Teeth slice

BATTLE STATS

ATTACK	Strength, claws, teeth 6/10
DEFENSE	Speed 5/10
X-FACTOR	Strong muscles 6/10

PREDATOR BATTLE RATING 75%

GIGANOTOSAURUS

The clue is in the name with this dinosaur. Giant Giganotosaurus was 41 feet long and weighed 8.8 tons. It looked like a larger version of T. rex, but Giganotosaurus lived in South America and T. rex in North America.

BONY HEAD
Bony lumps and ridges on the top of its head protected the skull and eyes from bumps. This would have made the head very heavy, and given that head was the size of a human being, it's a good thing Giganotosaurus had a strong neck.

BULLDOZER
With a body the size of Giganotosaurus, you don't really need weapons! This beast could simply body-slam its prey, pushing it to the ground and knocking it senseless.

ANY ARMS?
Under that huge body it was hard to see Giganotosaurus's tiny arms! They were short and weak, but long, sharp claws at the end of all six fingers meant it could swipe at prey when needed.

AIM BIG

Giganotosaurus liked to surprise its prey by bursting out of the tall South American trees. Sometimes it even took on the biggest of the giant plant-eating sauropods by teaming up with a family member.

DINO BATTLE
★ **CONTENDER No. 7** ★

NAME	GIGANOTOSAURUS
	(JIE-gah-not-oh-SORE-us)
LENGTH	41 feet
WEIGHT	8.8 tons
SPEED	19 mph

KEY ATTACKING MOVES
- Bite • Body slam

BATTLE STATS

ATTACK Teeth, jaws, body slam
surprise attack **10/10**

DEFENSE Size **8/10**

X-FACTOR Enormous size **8/10**

**PREDATOR
BATTLE RATING** 93%

DEINONYCHUS

This predator is all about speed. Small and light, it lived in what is now the USA during the Early Cretaceous Period. This creature looked a little like a bird, but with the deadly jaws of a meat-eating dinosaur.

RUN AND JUMP

The advantage of being small was that Deinonychus could leap into the air—you wouldn't see Giganotosaurus doing that! This predator would run toward prey bigger than itself and jump on its back. The claws could then inflict wounds, and Deinonychus's bite could finish the battle.

TOP SPEED

With a top speed of 35 mph, Deinonychus was a sprinter. It had strong leg muscles and a streamlined shape to allow it to run and attack prey like a bullet. Its long tail helped it balance when turning at speed.

SMALL, SHARP TEETH

Due to its size, Deinonychus did not have a strong bite. Instead, it had a mouth filled with lots of small, sharp teeth. Slotted close together, they could pierce flesh upon contact and cause a fatal wound for the prey.

DINO BATTLE
☆ CONTENDER No. 8 ☆

NAME	DEINONYCHUS
	(Die-nuh-NYE-kus)
LENGTH	9.8 feet
WEIGHT	132 pounds
SPEED	35 mph

KEY ATTACKING MOVES
• Speed • Jump

BATTLE STATS

ATTACK	Teeth, claws, jump 7/10
DEFENSE	Speed 8/10
X-FACTOR	Lightning-fast speed 9/10

PREDATOR BATTLE RATING **90%**

TERRIBLE CLAW

Deinonychus means "terrible claw," and this creature lives up to its name, with a huge, curved claw on the middle toe of each foot. The claw was used to pierce the skin of prey and then rip the flesh apart. Truly terrible!

CRYOLOPHOSAURUS

The predatory theropods of the Jurassic Period often looked alike. Cryolophosaurus stood out from the crowd, though, due to a special feature that could turn heads. Imagine coming face-to-face with those jaws, head crest, and horns!

COOL CARNIVORE

This dinosaur was one cool creature— its fossils were found just 404 miles from what is now the South Pole. It is the most southerly dinosaur ever discovered. But it wouldn't have been stomping about in the snow, since temperatures were warmer in the Early Jurassic Period than they are today.

TAIL WHIP

Cryolophosaurus had a long, thick tail that could knock out smaller prey with one flick. Almost as long as the dinosaur's body, it would also have helped balance the heavy head.

STRONG JAWS

Strong jaws filled with teeth would have been used to kill prey, as well as to devour animals that were already dead. Just because Cryolophosaurus had a killer instinct doesn't mean it would have passed up an easy meal!

ELVISAURUS

Cryolophosaurus had a stylish head crest that looked like a rock star's hairdo! It had distinctive grooves, was shaped like a fan, and was probably brightly colored to attract a mate—or else to create a scary territorial display to warn off rivals.

DINO BATTLE
☆ CONTENDER No. 9 ☆

NAME	CRYOLOPHOSAURUS *(CRY-oh-loaf-oh-SORE-us)*
LENGTH	19.7 feet
WEIGHT	992 pounds
SPEED	15 mph

KEY ATTACKING MOVES
- Bite • Tail swing

BATTLE STATS

ATTACK	Claws, teeth, strength	6/10
DEFENSE	Tail, head crest	7/10
X-FACTOR	Fan-shaped head crest	7/10

PREDATOR BATTLE RATING 78%

MAPUSAURUS

Fossils of Mapusaurus were excavated between 1997 and 2001 in Argentina. Scientists discovered a bone bed containing at least seven individuals, which suggests this mean predator hunted in packs.

GROUP WORK

Before discovering Mapusaurus, it was thought that all meat-eating dinosaurs hunted alone. The fact that Mapusaurus hunted in groups meant it had no limit on its choice of prey. Three of these crafty beasts could easily bring down a huge plant-eater—a real feast for the family!

TEETH LIKE KNIVES

Mapusaurus's teeth were designed for slicing through flesh rather than crushing bones. Its jaw was more delicate than T. rex's, suggesting that it preferred to wound prey and wait for it to die rather than killing it with a single bite.

LONG CLAWS

Mapusaurus had long, strong back legs but short arms. All its fingers and toes had a claw—the ones on its feet were used for kicking and stabbing, while the ones on its hands were used for grabbing and slicing.

BIG AND BULKY

At nearly 40 feet long, Mapusaurus was big—close to Giganotosaurus in size. Being built like a bus meant that it didn't have a high top speed, but it was solid and could easily shrug off any attackers.

NAME	MAPUSAURUS
	(MAP-uh-SORE-us)
LENGTH	39.4 feet
WEIGHT	6.6 tons
SPEED	15.5 mph

KEY ATTACKING MOVES

- Group attack • Claw swipe

BATTLE STATS

ATTACK	Teeth, claw swipe 6/10
DEFENSE	Size 8/10
X-FACTOR	Attacked as a group 8/10

PREDATOR BATTLE RATING

85%

ALLOSAURUS

This dinosaur was a common killer during the Late Jurassic Period. It was smart and built to attack smaller prey—at around 33 feet long, that meant it had a lot of choice!

FOOD, GLORIOUS FOOD

Allosaurus loved to eat meat and would stop at nothing to get a meal. It was a scavenger as well as a hunter. Favorite dishes included Camptosaurus, Stegosaurus, and young sauropods.

AMBUSH ATTACK

Being big meant that Allosaurus couldn't run at top speed for long. Its favorite method of attack was to ambush prey, taking it by surprise. This required just one quick tail swipe or body slam to knock prey down before going in for the kill.

AXE-LIKE SKULL

Allosaurus had a relatively weak bite, but its jaws were double-hinged, meaning it could open its mouth really wide. Its skull could withstand huge forces and it used its head like an ax.

NEW TEETH

Crunching through bones and eating huge chunks of meat meant that even the strongest of Allosaurus's curved teeth wore down over time. But it grew new teeth throughout its life, and if one tooth was knocked out in a fight, a new one soon grew to take its place.

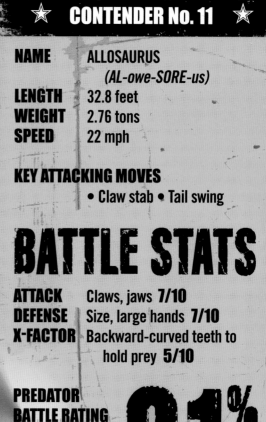

DINO BATTLE
★ CONTENDER No. 11 ★

NAME	ALLOSAURUS
	(AL-owe-SORE-us)
LENGTH	32.8 feet
WEIGHT	2.76 tons
SPEED	22 mph

KEY ATTACKING MOVES
• Claw stab • Tail swing

BATTLE STATS

ATTACK	Claws, jaws 7/10
DEFENSE	Size, large hands 7/10
X-FACTOR	Backward-curved teeth to hold prey 5/10

PREDATOR BATTLE RATING 81%

CARCHARODONTOSAURUS

This enormous killer was one to watch. Weighing in at over 7 tons and measuring about 43 feet, it was huge. Its teeth were its main weapon. At 6 inches long, serrated, and curved, there was nothing they couldn't cut through.

GREAT WHITE

Carcharodontosaurus's teeth look much like a great white shark's, and we all know what damage they can do! In fact, the first half of this dinosaur's name—*Carcharodon*—is the same as the great white shark's scientific name.

GOOD EYESIGHT

Dinosaurs had small brains and slow senses compared with human standards. But it is believed that Carcharodontosaurus had good stereoscopic vision, meaning it could use depth perception to figure out the distance between itself and its prey.

TERRITORIAL

A big dinosaur needs a big hunting range, but competition for the best patch of land was fierce. Rival males fought to secure their territory, and bite marks on the fossils of jawbones show they were prepared to fight to the death.

BATTLE TO BE THE BEST

Scientists think that Carcharodontosaurus would have fought with Spinosaurus. The two largest carnivores went head-to-head in the Middle Cretaceous Period. This was a battle of size and power against bite, and it was often too close to predict the outcome.

DINO BATTLE
★ CONTENDER No. 12 ★

NAME	CARCHARODONTOSAURUS
	(kahr-KAR-o-don-to-SORE-us)
LENGTH	42.7 feet
WEIGHT	7.7 tons
SPEED	19 mph

KEY ATTACKING MOVES

• Bite • Teeth slice

BATTLE STATS

ATTACK	Teeth, jaws	9/10
DEFENSE	Good eyesight, size	9/10
X-FACTOR	6-inch-long, serrated teeth	9/10

PREDATOR BATTLE RATING 95%

ALBERTOSAURUS

Albertosaurus was a top predator in western North America during the Late Cretaceous Period. It was smaller than its cousin T. rex, but more aerodynamic and flexible.

SLOW AND STEADY

Albertosaurus wasn't exactly slow, but it wasn't known for being fast. Instead, it was able to run longer distances than most of the large carnivores—a great advantage when competing for prey.

SEPTIC BITE

Like many dinosaurs, Albertosaurus had serrated teeth. Its teeth curved backward, though, meaning small pieces of meat may have stuck in the grooves and become home to deadly bacteria, giving it a septic bite.

TWO HORNS

The head had two blunt horns on it, which scientists believe may have helped to attract a mate. Even the scariest predators needed to find a partner to start a family and continue the survival of their species.

THIN JAWS

Like its body, Albertosaurus's jaws were smaller and thinner than T. rex's, but this gave it more precision and allowed it to slice prime pieces of meat off a carcass.

DINO BATTLE
★ CONTENDER No. 13 ★

NAME	ALBERTOSAURUS
	(Al-BER-to-SORE-us)
LENGTH	29.5 feet
WEIGHT	1.7 tons
SPEED	19 mph

KEY ATTACKING MOVES
- Bite • Teeth slice

BATTLE STATS

ATTACK	Jaws, group attack 8/10
DEFENSE	Able to run long distances 6/10
X-FACTOR	High stamina 6/10

PREDATOR BATTLE RATING

79%